Alfred's Basic Piano Library

Piano

Theory Through the Year

THEORY WORKSHEETS FOR USE IN PRIVATE OR GROUP LESSONS

Level 2

Alfred's Basic Piano Library, THEORY THROUGH THE YEAR, Level 2, is designed to be used with LESSON BOOK, Level 2. The books are coordinated page-by-page, with suggested assignments given in the upper right corner on each page of *Theory Through the Year.* This book reinforces the concepts taught in Theory Book, Level 2; it can be used effectively as a supplement for other methods as well.

Each page in the book has a holiday, monthly or seasonal theme. The book was written to serve as a motivational tool for reviewing important concepts (note reading, music symbols and terms, note values, rhythms) throughout the entire year. Consequently, each page should be used at the appropriate time of the year *after* the student has completed the corresponding page in the LESSON BOOK.

The book may be used in private lessons, group lessons and summer piano camps. Because its concepts are presented in a game-like format, this book lets students have fun while learning THEORY THROUGH THE YEAR!

June C. Montgomery

Illustrated by Liana Kelley and Beverly Lazor-Bahr

Use after ALFRED'S BASIC PIANO LIBRARY, Lesson Book 2, page 3.

Paper and Pencils

On each pad write the indicated music symbol.

Choose your answers from the symbols in the pencil holder.

Use after page 5.

Apples for the Teacher

Add the rhythmic value of the notes in each apple slice.
Write the answer on the line.

Use after page 7.

Helmets and Jerseys

Name the notes in each helmet.
Draw a line to connect each helmet with the matching jersey.

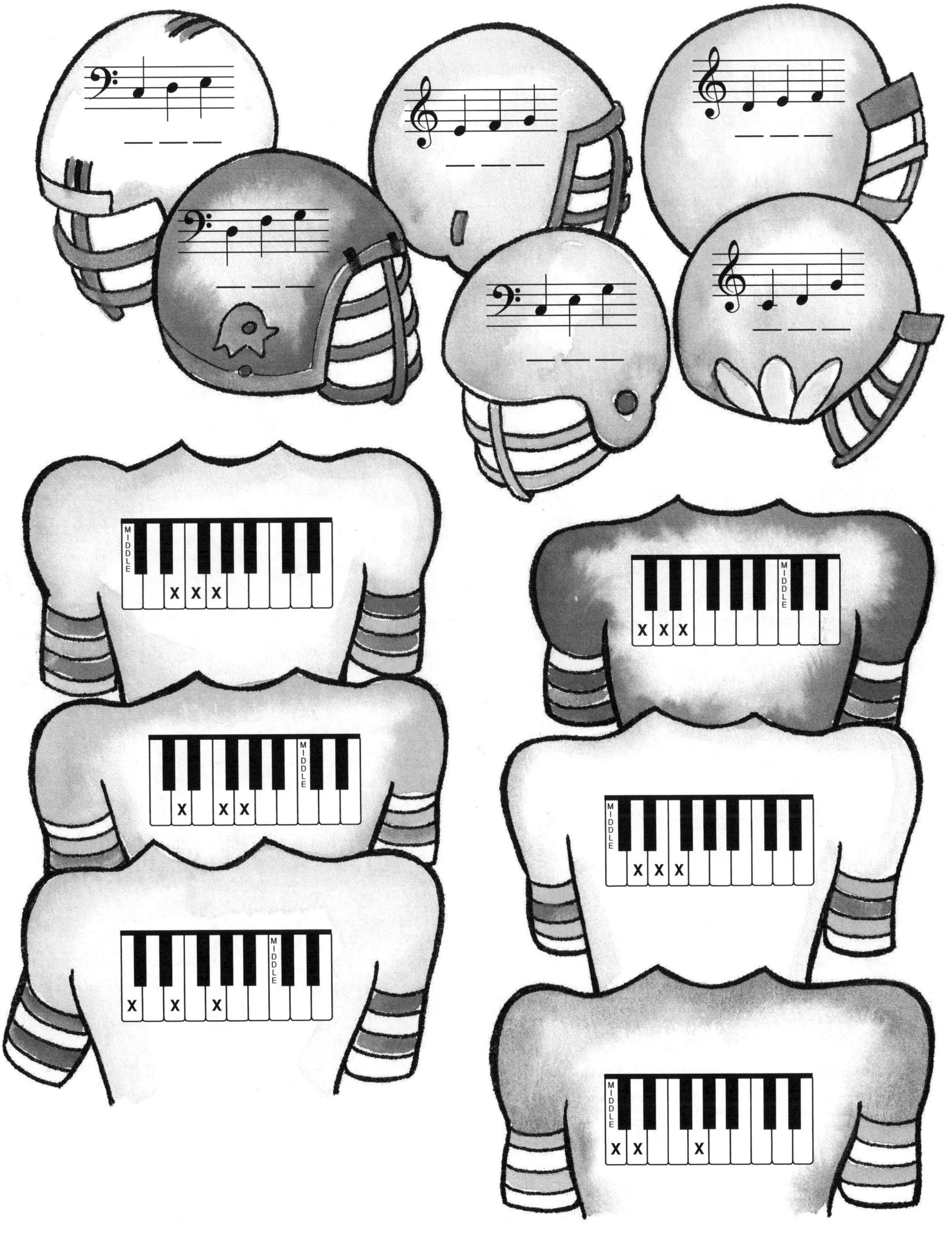

Use after page 11.

Pumpkins and Gourds

On the keyboard inside each pumpkin, write the missing key name for the melodic interval indicated. Draw a line from each pumpkin to the TWO gourds that contain the same melodic interval.

Use after page 13.

Notes and Ghosts

In each ghost, write the note names in the boxes. On the line, write the interval number. Indicate if the interval is melodic or harmonic by circling the M or H in the ghost's hand.

Use after page 17.

Turkey Puzzle

Complete the sentences below; then solve the crossword puzzle. Choose your answers from the words surrounding the puzzle.

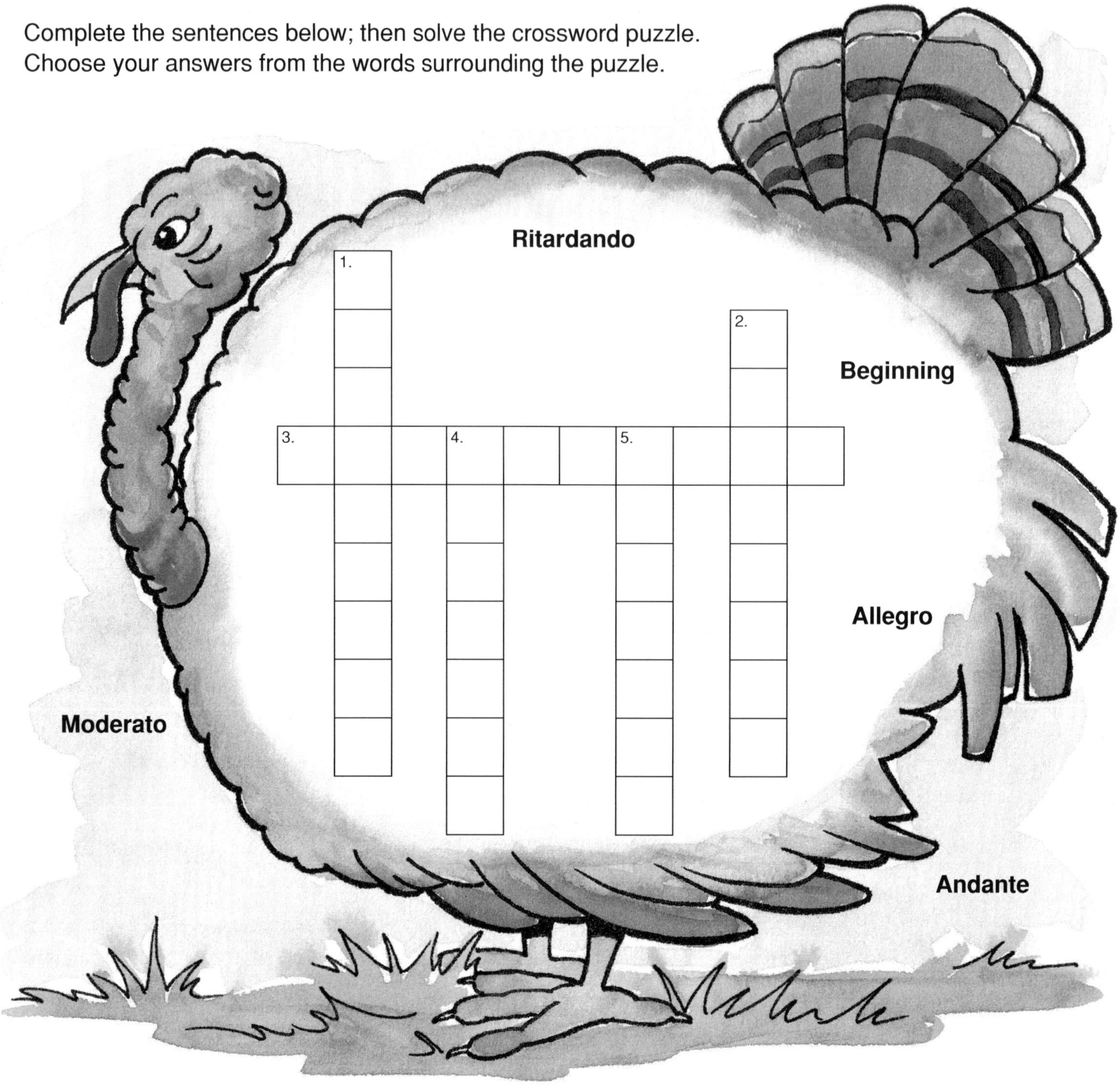

CLUES

Down:

1. *D. C. al Fine* means to repeat from the ______________________ and play to the *Fine.*
2. ______________________ means to play with a moderate speed.
4. ______________________ means to play quickly and happily.
5. ______________________ means to play at a walking speed; moving along.

Across:

3. ______________________ means to play gradually slower.

Use after page 19.

Harvest Time

Using the note value at the top of each haystack, fill in each box by writing the note, rest and number of counts.

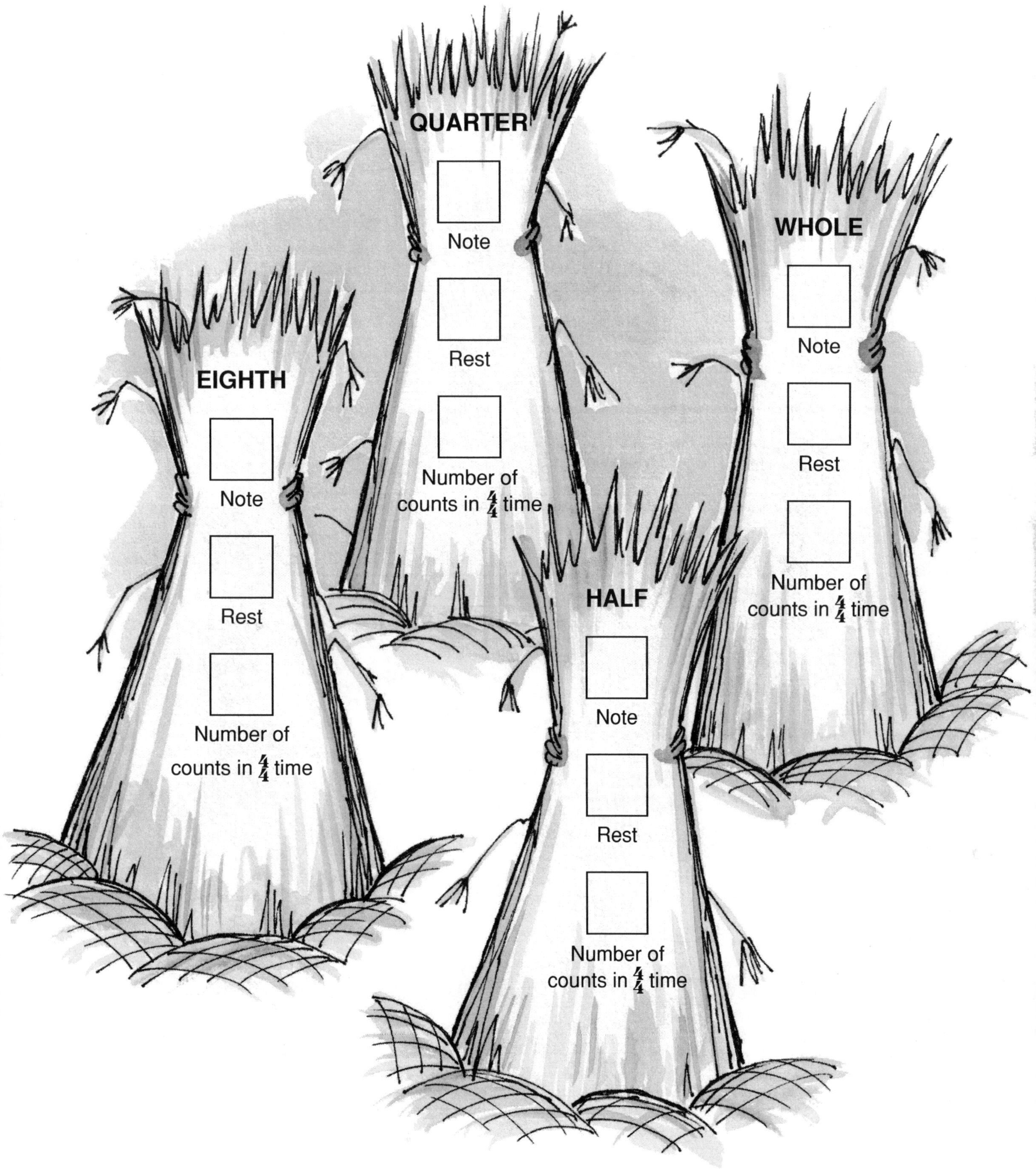

Use after page 21.

Christmas Cookies

Draw a line from the star cookies to the matching tree cookies.

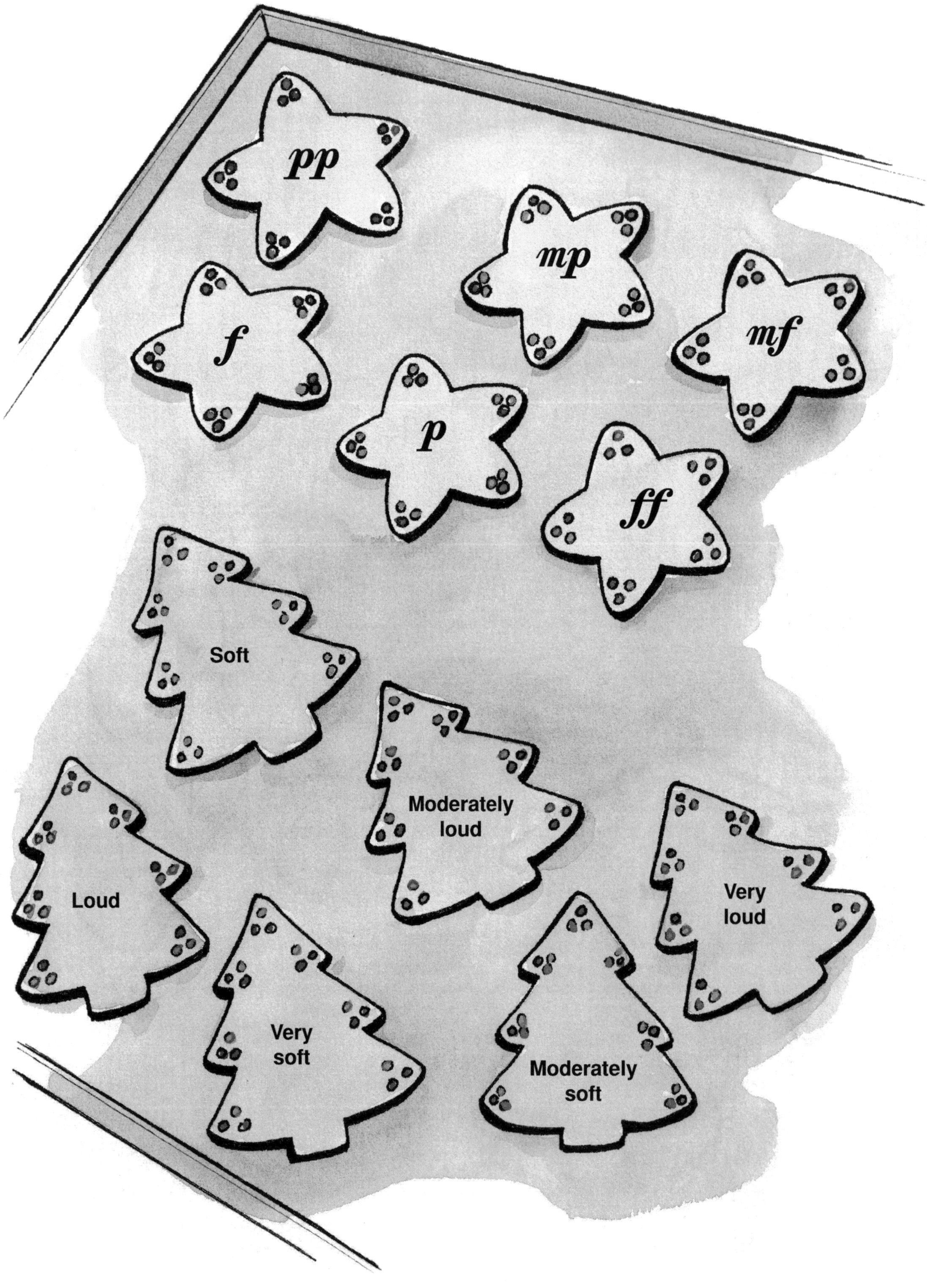

Use after page 23.

Christmas Stockings

On each keyboard in the mantle, write the letter name on the key that is an interval of a 7th above the given note.

Write the interval number in the foot of each stocking.

Indicate whether the interval is melodic or harmonic by circling the correct bell.

Use after page 25.

Toboggans

On the keyboard on the hill, write the letter names of the notes of the C MAJOR SCALE.
On the lines, write W for whole step or H for half step.

On the keyboard in each toboggan, write the finger numbers of the C MAJOR SCALE ASCENDING (going up) in the left hand and DESCENDING (going down) in the right hand. Circle the keys where 3 crosses over 1.

Use after page 27.

New Year Party

In each party hat, write the note names in the boxes. On the line, write the interval number. Indicate whether the interval is melodic or harmonic by circling the M or H in the ribbons.

Use after page 29.

Be My Valentine

On the large keyboard, write the letter names of the notes of the G MAJOR SCALE.
On the lines, write W for whole step or H for half step.

On the smaller keyboards, write the finger numbers of the G MAJOR SCALE ASCENDING (going up) in the left hand and DESCENDING (going down) in the right hand. Circle the keys where 3 crosses over 1.

Use after page 33.

Hearts and Flowers

Color each heart and its matching flower the same color. You will need six colors.

Use after page 35.

Cherries for George

Add two notes to the 1st, 4th and 5th notes of the scale to build the PRIMARY TRIADS in C MAJOR.

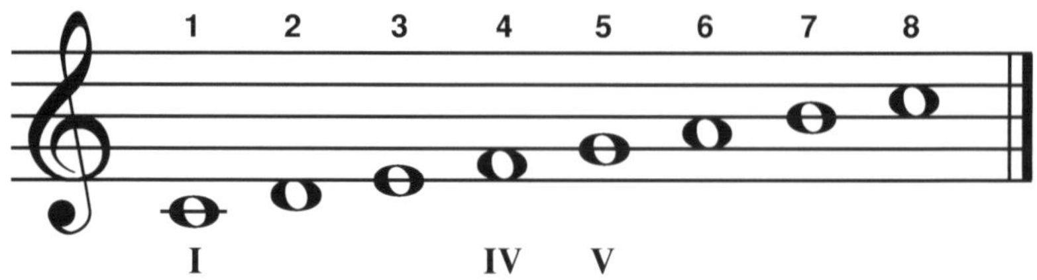

For the bass clef examples in the cherries below, write the name of the ROOT of the triad.
For the treble clef examples, write the ROMAN NUMERAL of each triad in the key of C MAJOR.

Use after page 37.

The Leprechaun

Using the following steps, build a G^7 chord.

Inside the coins on the leprechaun, write the letter names of the keys marked with a black "X." Then write the notes on the staff, above the given note.

STEP 1
Begin with a G major triad in ROOT POSITION.

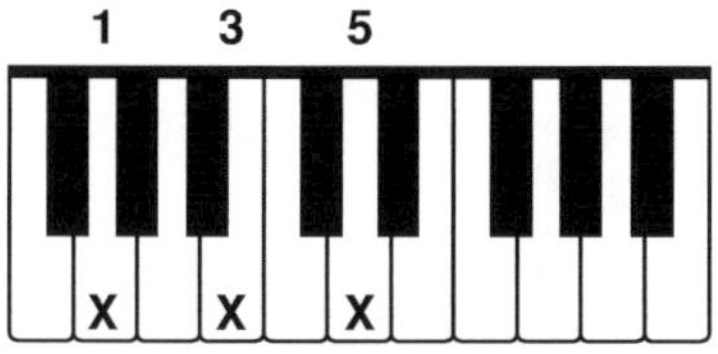

STEP 2
Add a note a 7th above the root.

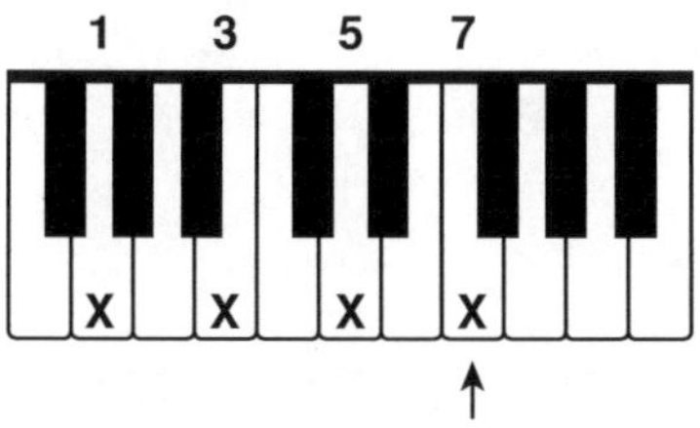

STEP 3
Move the root up an octave.

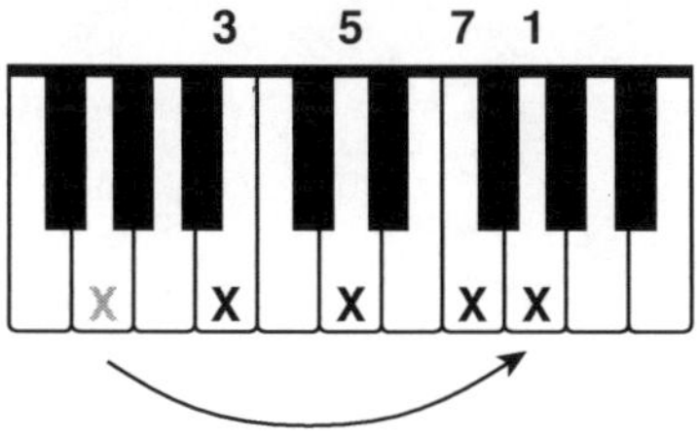

STEP 4
Omit the 5th.

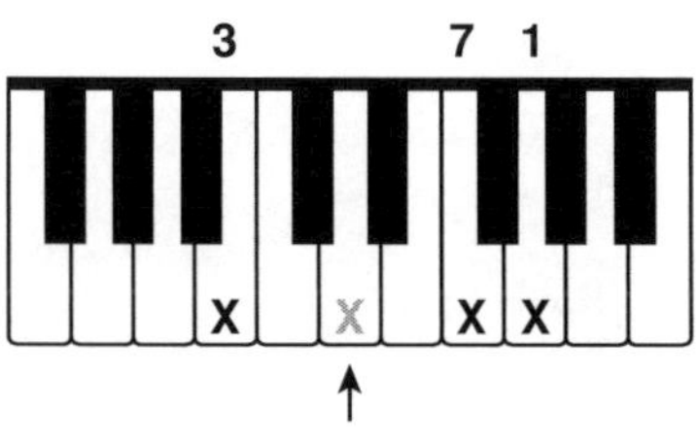

Use after page 39.

Spring's in the Air

Add one rest to complete the measures in each kite and cloud.
Then clap and count the rhythms.

Use after page 41.

First Come the Tulips

Using the following steps, build a D⁷ chord.

Inside the tulips, write the names of the keys marked with a black "X."
Then write the notes on the staff above the given note.

STEP 1
Begin with a D major triad
in ROOT POSITION.

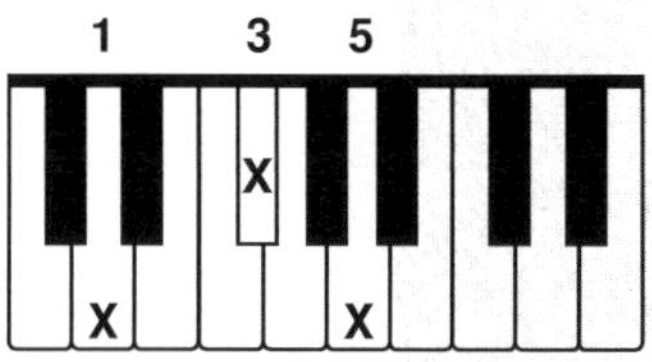

STEP 2
Add a note a 7th
above the root.

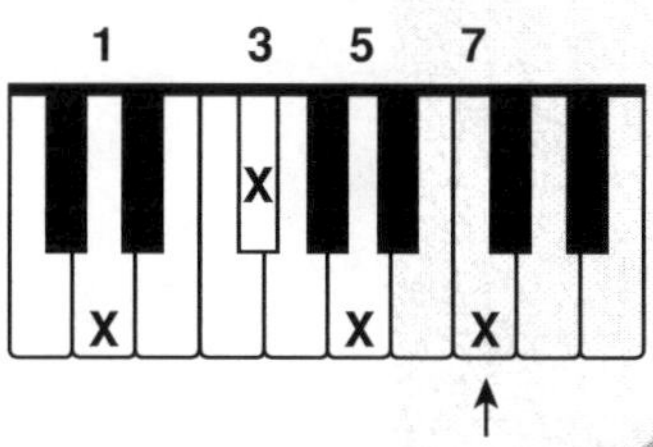

STEP 3
Move the root up
an octave.

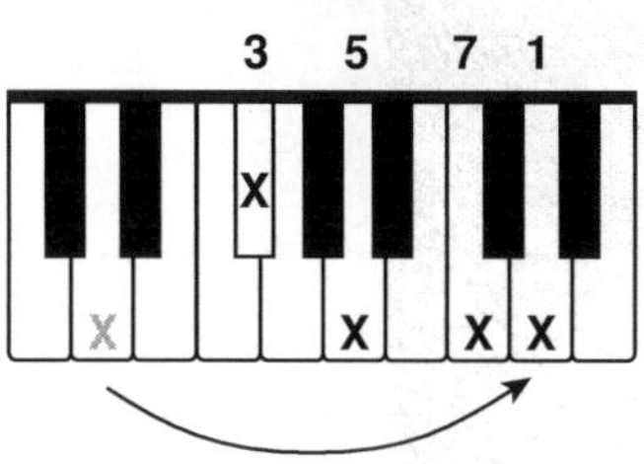

STEP 4
Omit the 5th.

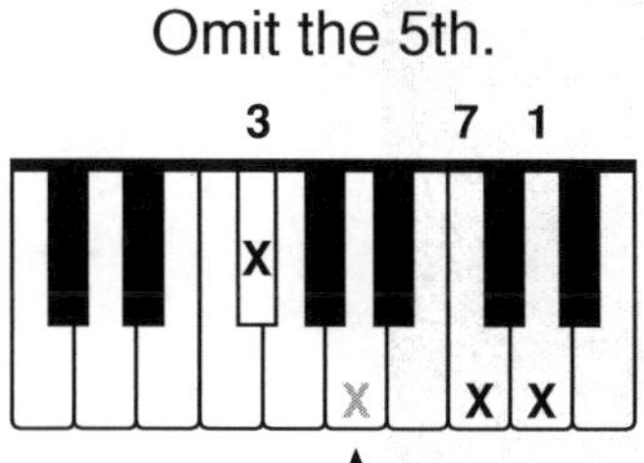

Use after page 43.

Easter Basket

On the keyboard in the basket, write the letter names of the notes of the D MAJOR SCALE. On the lines, write W for whole step or H for half step.

On the keyboards in the rabbits, write the finger numbers of the D MAJOR SCALE ASCENDING (going up) in the left hand and DESCENDING (going down) in the right hand. Circle the keys where 3 crosses over 1.

Use after page 45.

Plant a Tree

Using the following steps, build an A^7 chord.

On the leaves of the tree, write the names of the keys marked with a black "X." Then write the notes on the staff above the given note.

STEP 1
Begin with an A major triad in ROOT POSITION.

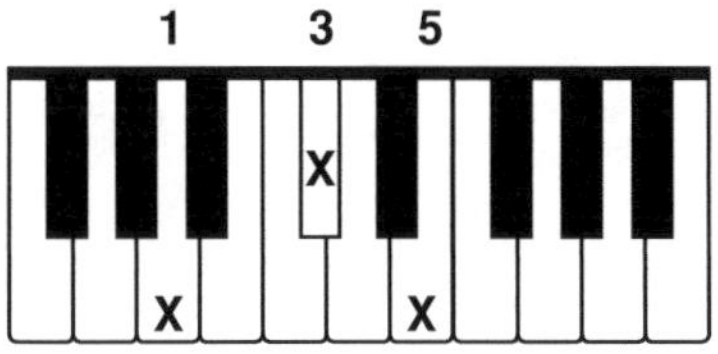

STEP 2
Add a note a 7th above the root.

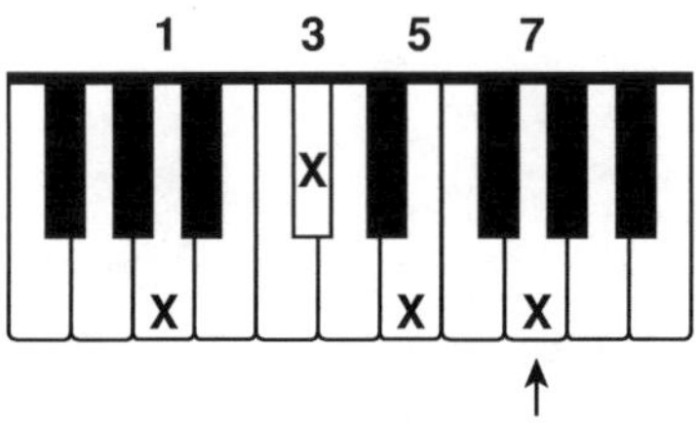

STEP 3
Move the root up an octave.

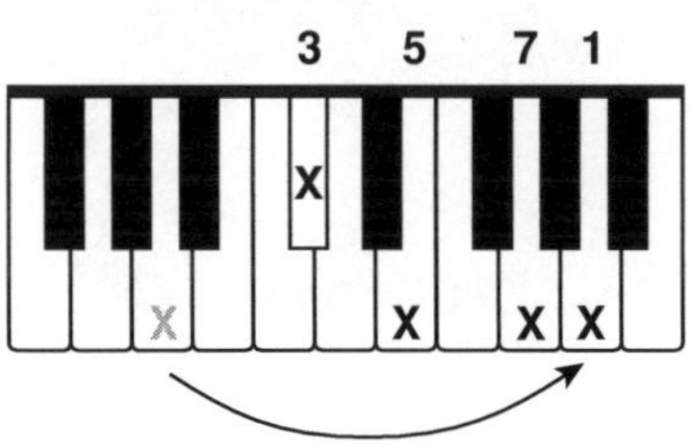

STEP 4
Omit the 5th.

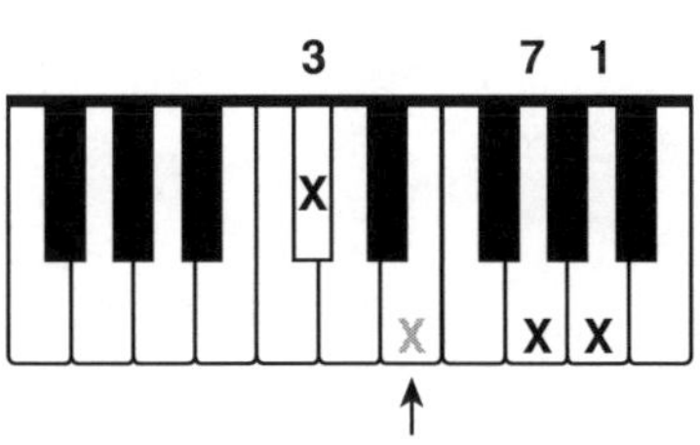

The chords in the grass are the 3 PRIMARY CHORDS IN D MAJOR.
Connect the chords to their matching ROMAN NUMERAL.

Use after page 47.

Surf Season

Color the section of each surfboard that is in the key of C major YELLOW.
Color the section that is in the key of G major RED.
Color the section that is in the key of D major ORANGE.

Each surfboard will contain the three colors.

Water Slides

Use after page 47.

Draw a line connecting each music example to its matching ball in the pool.

Use after page 47.

Fourth Celebration

In the fireworks, write the interval numbers in the boxes below the staff.
Circle the FOURTHS.

In the boats:

- Write the chord letter name.
- Write the Roman numeral.
- Write the name of the key.
- Circle the IV chords.